For Izzy

DK
LONDON, NEW YORK,
MELBOURNE, MUNICH, and DELHI

BLAST LAB
Secret Agent

Designed by Jess Bentall
Design assistant Lauren Rosier
Edited by Alexander Cox
Science consultants Francis Bate and Donald Franceschetti
Photography Andy Crawford
Production editor Clare McLean
Jacket editor Mariza O'Keeffe

First published in Great Britain in 2009 by
Dorling Kindersley Limited,
80 Strand, London, WC2R 0RL

2 4 6 8 10 9 7 5 3 1
BD721 – 10/09

A CIP catalogue record for this book is available
from the British Library

ISBN: 978-1-40534-084-7

Printed and bound by L Rex Printing Co. Ltd, China

Picture Credits: The publisher would like to thank the following for their kind permission to reproduce their photographs: (Key: a-above; b-below/bottom; c-centre; f-far; l-left; r-right; t-top) 8 **iStockphoto.com:** Ivar Teunissen (cla/sticker). 9 **iStockphoto.com:** mammamaart (fclb/sticker) All other images © Dorling Kindersley. For further information see: www.dkimages.com

A SEPTEMBER FILMS PRODUCTION in association with
HAMSTER'S WHEEL PRODUCTIONS as seen on BBC.

Discover more at
www.dk.com

Eye See You

AS A SECRET AGENT, you'll need to keep an eye on the enemy, using clever GADGETS. Fear not – here's how to make your own SPY-EYE PERISCOPE.

Can you see round corners?

Periscopes help you see above high obstacles like fences and walls. You can even use them sideways and peer round corners!

Spy science explained!

LIGHT RAYS always travel in straight lines. Mirrored surfaces, like the pieces of card in our periscope, bounce light rays back out at EXACTLY THE SAME ANGLE that they arrive, so that you see a reflection.

The mirrors in the periscope are angled at 45 degrees, which is the perfect angle to bounce light from one mirror onto the other, and then into your eye.

Sneaky sight

Periscopes are used by submarines to look above the waves without giving away their position to enemy ships. The first periscope was used on a submarine in 1902.

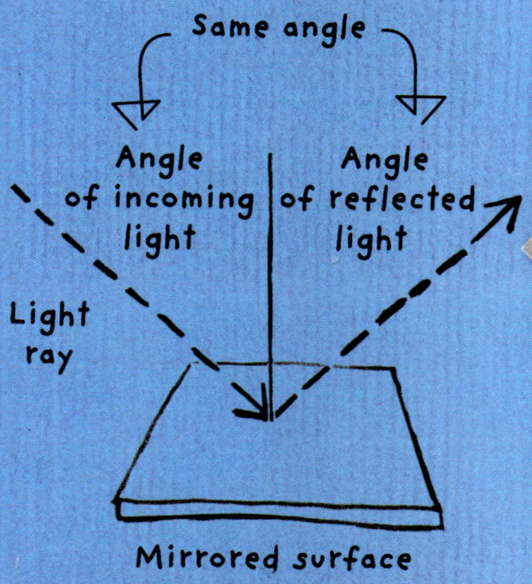

HOW TO MAKE A PERISCOPE

All you need is...

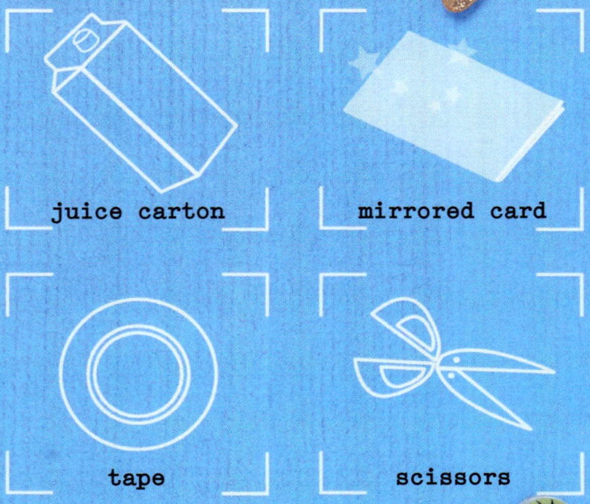

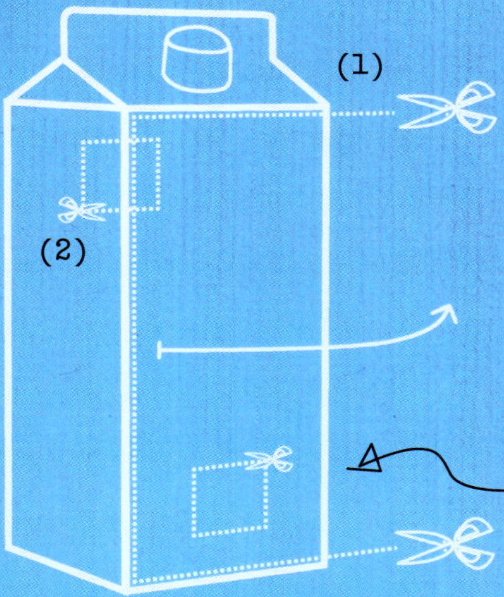

(1) Cut along three sides of the carton to open it up.

(2) At the top of one side, cut an eye-sized hole. This is the viewhole.

Then cut another hole at the bottom of the opposite side. This is the eyehole.

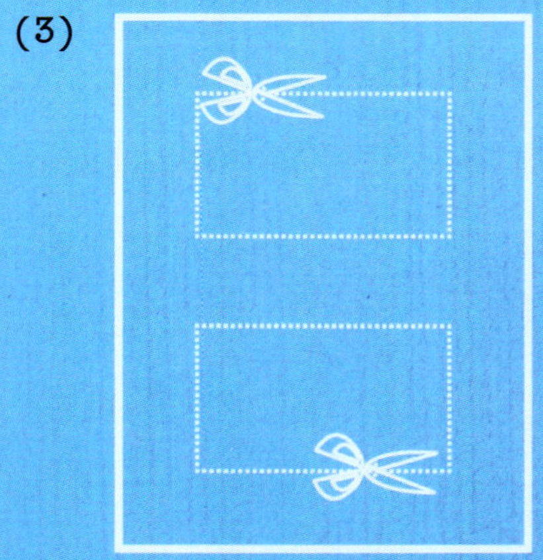

(3) Cut two rectangles of mirrored card. Don't cut them too small.

(4) Place a rectangle of mirrored card into the bottom of the carton at a 45 degree angle. Then do the same for the mirrored card at the top of the carton...

... Tape both pieces of card in place. The mirrored sides should face each other.

(5) Close up the carton with tape. If your angles are correct, you can look in the eyehole and see out of the viewhole!

If not, change the angles of the card until you can.

N.B. Don't use permanent pens!

Secret Pen!

SOMETIMES SPIES SEND secret messages to each other. Here's how to find out WHOSE PEN was used to write the secret note.

HOW TO FIND THE PEN

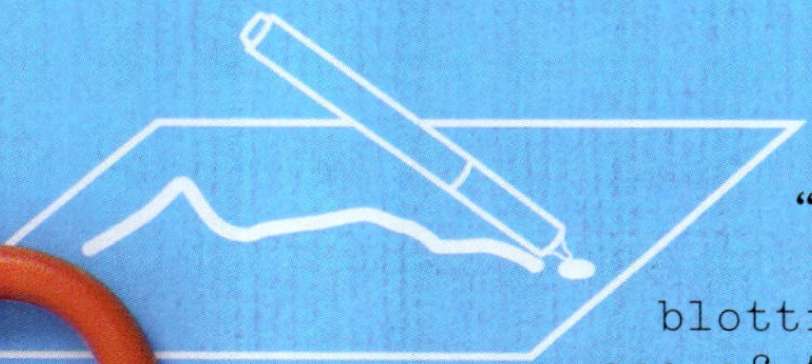

(1) Ask a friend to secretly write "SECRET..." on a piece of blotting paper with one of the three felt pens. Remember the full stops!

(2) Cut three strips of blotting paper, about the depth of the tub.

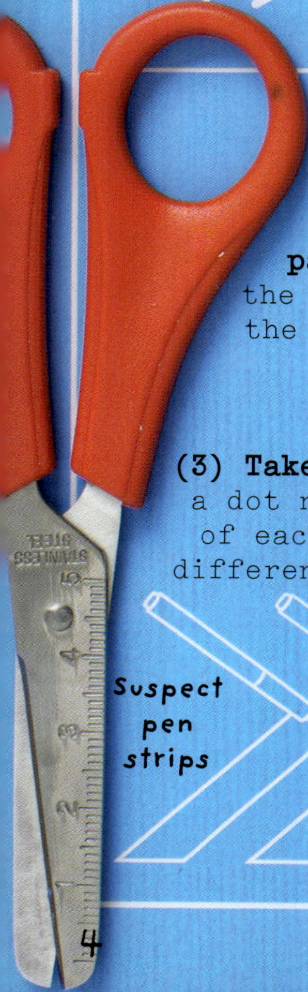

(3) Take a pen and make a dot near the bottom of each strip. Use a different pen for each.

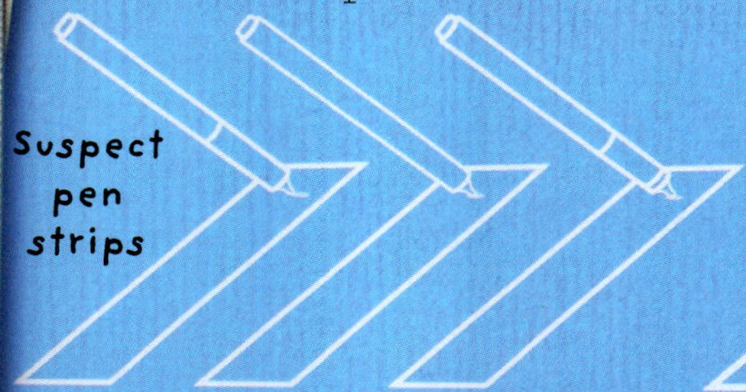

(4) Cut a strip out of the "SECRET..." note. Use a full stop as your dot for the test.

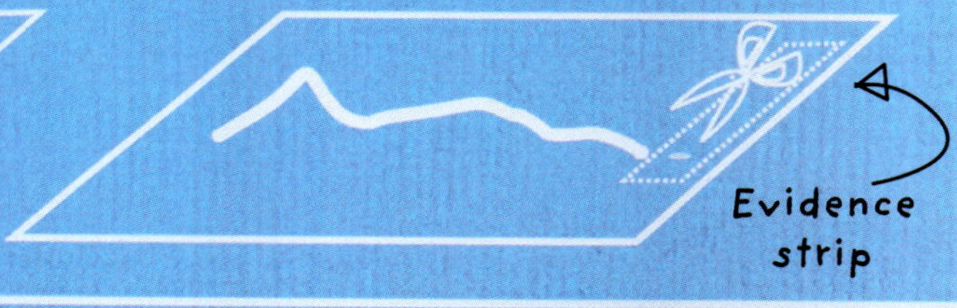

All you need is...

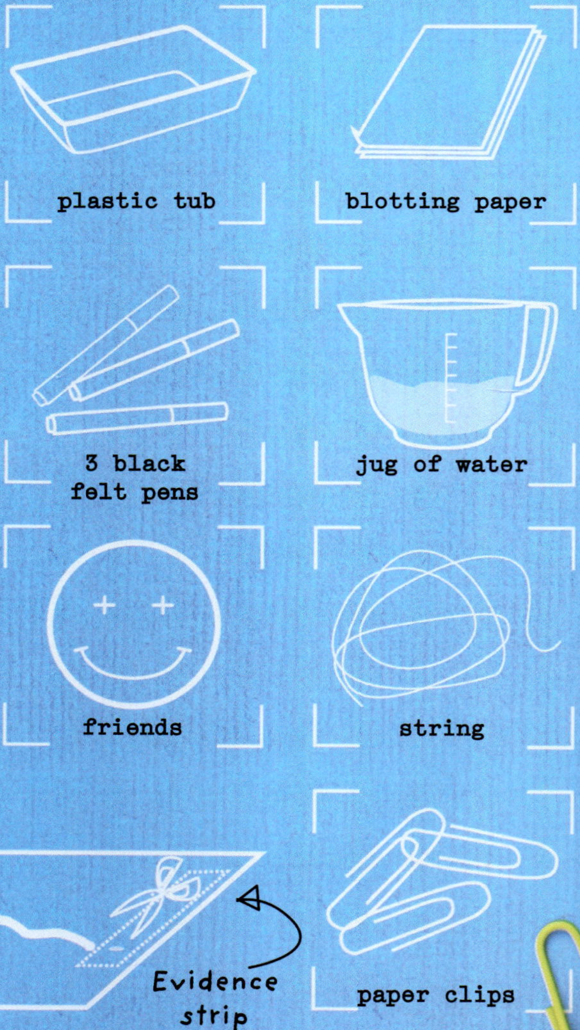

Use three different makes of felt pen.

(5) Fix some string across the top of the plastic tub – for example using sticky tape – so it looks like a tightrope. Fill the tub with water to a depth of 1 cm (½ in).

(6) Paper clip each strip to the string, so that the very end of the strip (but not the dot) hangs into the water.

Evidence strip

(7) Leave for 10 minutes to allow the blotting paper to absorb water.

Spy science explained!

The ink in black felt pens is a mixture of different coloured chemicals. Some chemicals dissolve easier in water and spread up the blotting paper, creating a unique colour pattern.

Your evidence strip is a colourful "pen-print" that you can use to identify the secret pen!

Now compare the "pen-print" of each suspect strip to the original evidence strip. You should now know which is the guilty pen!

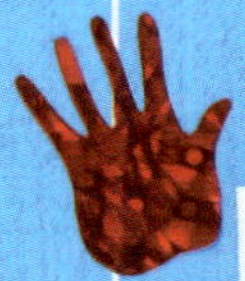

Finding Prints

A CARELESS CRIMINAL can leave clues at a crime scene. A fingerprint can be a key piece of EVIDENCE – so get dusting!

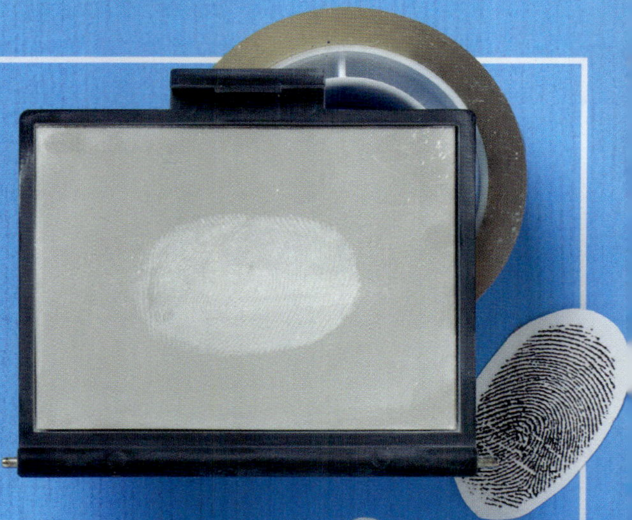

This one's been dusted already.

HOW TO DUST FOR PRINTS

All you need is...

(1) Press your finger firmly on the mirror.

(2) Dip the brush in talcum powder, shake off the excess powder, then use the brush to dust the mirror.

Make sure you dust carefully, so you don't smudge the print.

(3) Take a strip of tape, and gently stick it over the white fingerprint. Slowly peel it off.

(4) Stick the tape on the black card. Now you can see the fingerprint in detail!

TOP SECRET

CONFIDENTIAL

SECRET FILES

CRIME SCENE DO NOT CROSS CRIME SCENE DO NOT CROSS

CRIME SCENE DO NOT CROSS CRIME SCENE DO NOT CROSS

TOP SECRET

CONFIDENTIAL

SECRET FILES

CRIME SCENE DO NOT CROSS CRIME SCENE DO NOT CROSS

CRIME SCENE DO NOT CROSS CRIME SCENE DO NOT CROSS

Making Prints

YOU'VE FOUND FINGERPRINTS. But they are only useful if you can compare them. That means INKY fingers!

There are THREE types of fingerprint.

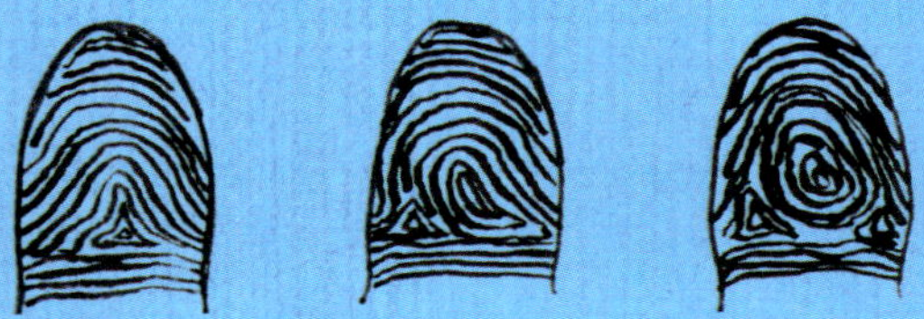

ARCH WHORL LOOP

HOW TO INK PRINTS

All you need is...

ink pad

white card

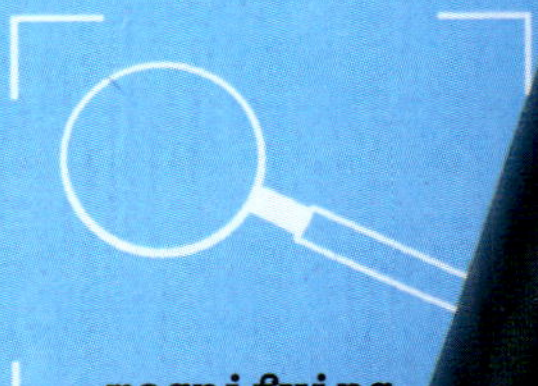

magnifying glass

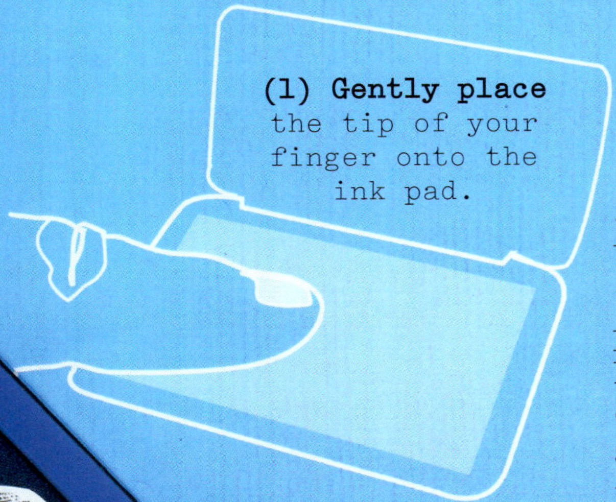

(1) Gently place the tip of your finger onto the ink pad.

(2) Now gently press your finger on the white card. Don't smudge it!

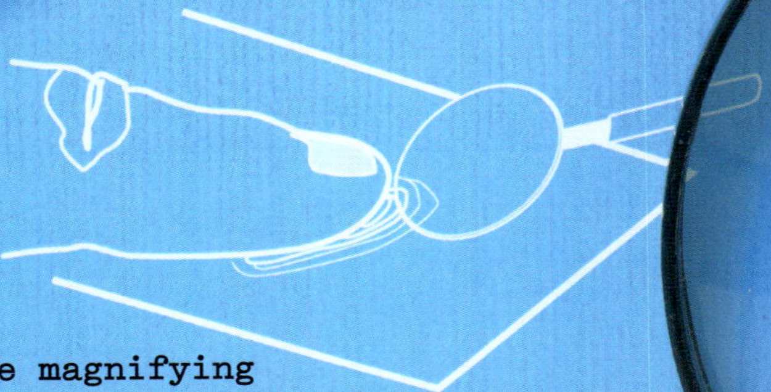

(3) Use the magnifying glass to look at the hoops and loops of the print.

Spy science

Your hands are covered in tiny grooves, which provide friction and help you grip. To add extra grip, skin oils are channelled along the grooves. It's these oils that leave the outline of the fingerprint on shiny surfaces.

Stay out of my room!

Intruder Alert!

AS A SPY, you'll need to keep top-secret files from ENEMY AGENTS. Protect your bedroom with an INTRUDER ALARM!

HOW TO MAKE AN ALARM

All you need is...

scissors

musical card

book

fishing wire

(1) Peel back the piece of cardboard that is hiding all the electrical parts in the musical card.

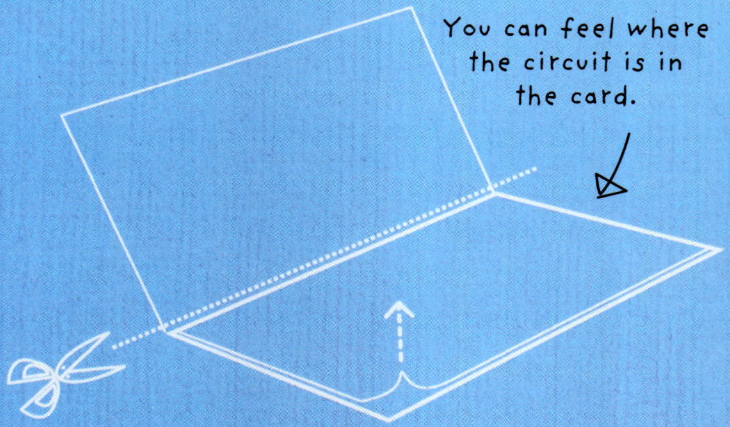

(2) There should be a small plastic strip in the crease of the card. Carefully detach it. Tie the fishing wire around the end of the strip.

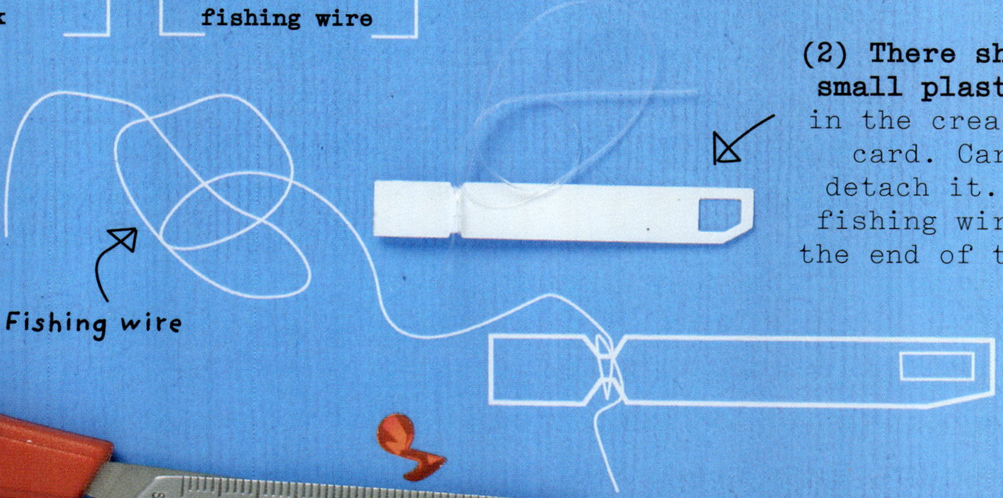

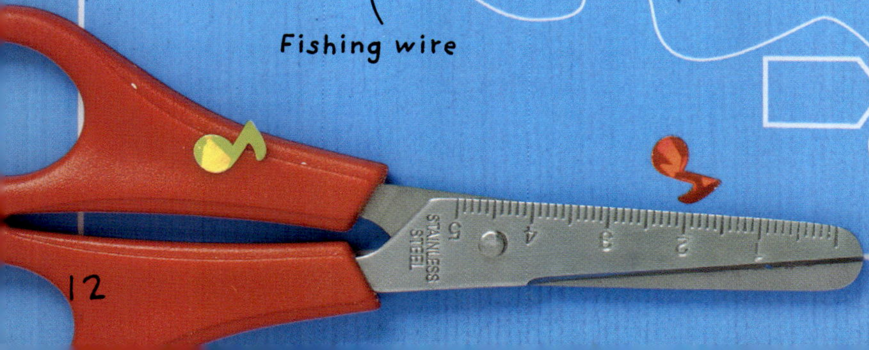

KEEP OUT!

SUPER-SPY TOP TIP
You have to position the intruder alarm just right. Make sure that when the door opens it tugs on the fishing wire, and pulls the plastic strip out of the pincer.

Spy science explained!

The mechanism in the card is an electrical circuit connecting a battery to a speaker. When the plastic strip is in the pincer, it stops the flow of electricity, so the buzzer doesn't sound. But when the door opens, it pulls the strip from the pincer, and this completes the electrical circuit. The speaker converts electricity to sound: INTRUDER ALERT!

(3) Cut away the rest of the card so you are left with just the circuit board and speaker.

(4) Attach the loose end of the fishing wire to your bedroom door handle.

(5) Locate the metal pincer on the circuit board.

(6) Carefully, hook the hole on the plastic strip under the pincer.

(7) Now hide the circuit board and speaker in a heavy book, and make sure the fishing line is taut. You're ready for any intruders!

DNA Extraction

Spy missions can be challenging. Do you want to SEE WHAT YOU'RE MADE OF? Now you can – let's EXTRACT some DNA.

Your DNA is completely unique to you, unless you're an identical twin.

All you need is...

HOW TO EXTRACT YOUR DNA

(1) Put the nail varnish remover in the freezer for 10 minutes.

(2) Take a clean glass and add three teaspoons of tap water...

... then add one teaspoon of washing-up liquid.

You can keep your DNA in a pot or a test tube and show it to your mates!

It tastes pretty disgusting!

(3) Take a mouthful of salty water and swill it around your mouth.

(4) Now, spit the salty water into the glass of washing-up liquid and water. Swish the mixture around in the glass for five minutes.

A single hair, or a drop of blood or saliva can be used as DNA evidence in an investigation.

(5) Slowly pour some nail varnish remover into the glass, so it forms a layer on top.

(6) After five minutes, white strands will appear in the layer of nail varnish remover. Use the kebab sticks to fish these out – they are made of your DNA!

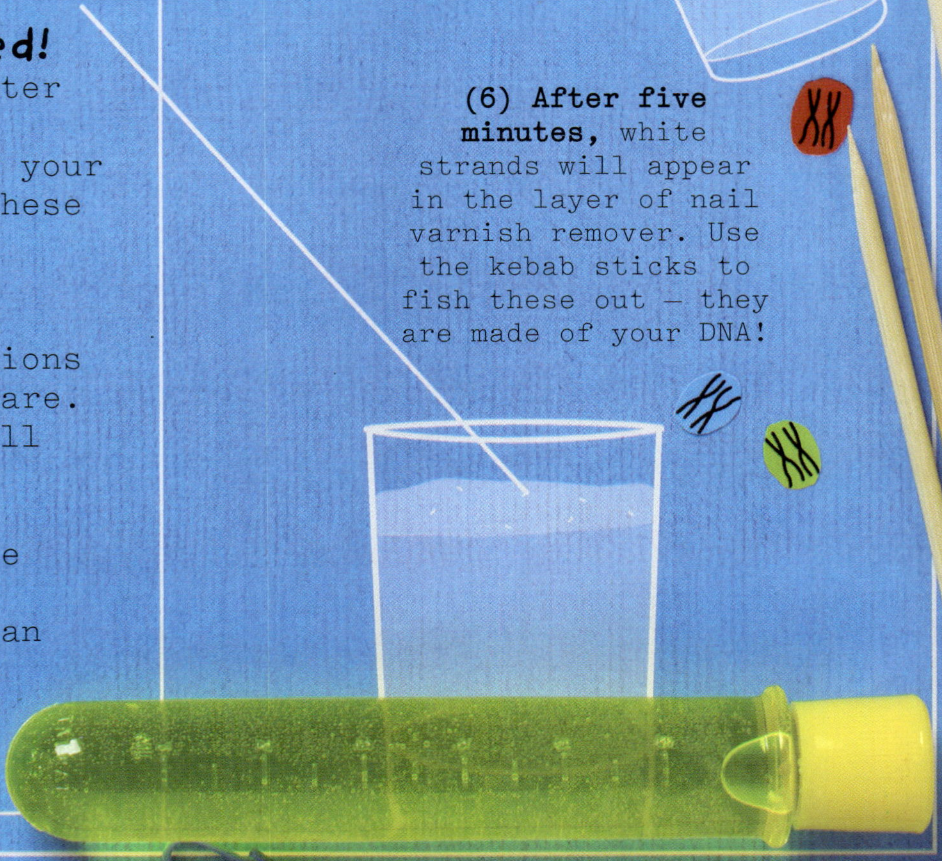

Spy science explained!

When you swill salty water in your mouth, you're washing tiny cells from your cheeks and gums – and these cells contain DNA.

What is DNA? DNA is the set of genetic instructions that makes you who you are. It is found in every cell of your body.

Everyone's DNA is unique (except for identical twins). Investigators can use DNA evidence from a crime scene to find and convict criminals.

Secret Agent Quiz

1. The code for human DNA consists of four letters – A, C, G, and T. But how many letters long is the human genetic code?

a. 300 letters
b. 3000 letters
c. 3 million letters
d. 3 billion letters

2. The curves and creases in a fingerprint are given names relating to their shape. Which of the below is not a type of fingerprint?

a. Arch
b. Loop
c. Hoop
d. Whorl

3. Night-vision goggles are a must for any spy. But what type of light do they detect to help spies see in the dark?

a. Twilight
b. Infrared light
c. Cosmic light
d. Ultra-blue light

4. During World War 2, the Germans developed a code machine called Enigma. It was really hard to crack. How many different ways could each letter in a message be encoded?

a. 15 billion billion
b. 15 million
c. 15,000
d. 15

ANSWERS: (1) d. 3 billion letters long; (2) c. Arch, loop, and whorl are all real fingerprint types. Which do you have? (3) b. Humans see within a small range called visible light. Night vision increases what we see into other ranges, including infrared light. (4) a. 15,000,000,000,000,000,000. After a few errors from the Germans, it still took the Allies years to crack Enigma (and they used a computer)!